Analysis of the Sandy Recovery Improvement Act of 2013

Jared T. Brown
Analyst in Emergency Management and Homeland Security Policy

Francis X. McCarthy
Analyst in Emergency Management Policy

Edward C. Liu
Legislative Attorney

March 11, 2013

Congressional Research Service

7-5700

www.crs.gov

R42991

CRS Report for Congress ————————————————

Prepared for Members and Committees of Congress

Summary

Hurricane Sandy caused extensive human suffering and damage to public and private property. In response to this catastrophic event, Congress considered legislation to provide supplemental appropriations to federal disaster assistance programs. In addition, Congress considered revisions to the Robert T. Stafford Disaster Relief and Emergency Assistance Act (the Stafford Act, P.L. 93-288 as amended), which is the primary source of authorities for disaster assistance programs for the Federal Emergency Management Agency (FEMA). As a result, Congress passed the Sandy Recovery Improvement Act of 2013, which was included as Division B of the Disaster Relief Appropriations Act, 2013 (P.L. 113-2). Division A of P.L. 113-2 provided a $50.7 billion package of disaster assistance largely focused on responding to Hurricane Sandy. Additionally, Congress increased the National Flood Insurance Program's borrowing authority by $9.7 billion (from $20.725 billion to $30.425 billion) (P.L. 113-1). Both of these supplemental relief law are discussed separately in CRS Report R42869, *FY2013 Supplemental Funding for Disaster Relief*.

This report analyzes the provisions of the Sandy Recovery Improvement Act of 2013. In general, these provisions amend the Stafford Act with a stated goal of improving the efficiency and quality of disaster assistance provided by FEMA. Briefly, the amendments to the Stafford Act include:

- Establishing a new set of alternative procedures for administering the Public Assistance Program, which provides assistance for debris removal and the repair and restoration of eligible facilities (Section 1102 of the Sandy Recovery Improvement Act of 2013);

- Authorizing FEMA to enter into agreements with private owners of multi-family rental properties to expand post-disaster housing resources (Section 1103);

- Revising the administration of the Hazard Mitigation Grant Program, to include a possible advancement of 25% of grant funds (Section 1104);

- Directing the establishment of alternative dispute resolution procedures (including binding arbitration), building on FEMA's current appeals process, to resolve federal and state disagreements on costs and eligibility questions (Section 1105);

- Directing the creation of a joint process for environmental and historical review for disaster recovery projects with the goal of increasing the speed of the process (Section 1106);

- Directing FEMA to study, and report to Congress, whether it is appropriate to increase the dollar size of "small projects" eligible for simplified procedures (Section 1107);

- Including child care as an eligible expense under the "other needs assistance" provided in certain disasters (Section 1108(a));

- Specifically authorizing the reimbursement of the base wages of government employees providing emergency work under certain circumstances (Section 1108(b));

- Directing FEMA to update the factors considered when assessing the need for Individual Assistance in the declaration process (Section 1109);

- Authorizing the chief executive of a tribal government to directly request disaster or emergency declarations from the President, much as a governor can for a state (Section 1110); and

- Directing FEMA to create a comprehensive national strategy for reducing the cost of future disasters (Section 1111).

Prospectively, the changes in law apply to disasters declared on or after the date of enactment, January 29, 2013. Further, support can be found in the text and legislative history of the bill for applying at least some of these amendments retrospectively to Hurricane Sandy-related disaster declarations. However, it is less clear whether, and to what extent, some of these revisions will apply to disasters declared before Hurricane Sandy.

This report will be updated as events warrant.

Contents

Tables

Appendixes

Contacts

Introduction

Given its size, strength, location and the enormity of its impact, Hurricane Sandy was a storm of historic proportions and importance. The damage inflicted by this huge storm rivaled the damages of the Gulf Coast storms during the summer of 2005, particularly due to the population density and overall development of the areas that received the brunt of the storm's impact. As with other major natural disaster events, Members of Congress responded to Hurricane Sandy by holding a series of hearings, visiting the affected region, and introducing and acting on legislation.

In addition to evaluating the need for supplemental appropriations in response to this catastrophic disaster, the 112th and 113th Congresses considered reforming provisions of the Robert T. Stafford Disaster Relief and Emergency Assistance Act (the Stafford Act, P.L. 93-288 as amended).[1] Generally, concerns were raised that the recovery from Hurricane Sandy would be plagued by perceived delays and bureaucratic burdens that inhibited the recovery following Hurricane Katrina. The Sandy Recovery Improvement Act of 2013, as passed as Division B of P.L. 113-2, the Disaster Relief Appropriations Act, 2013, revises the Stafford Act as a result of these concerns as well as other considerations. Division A of P.L. 113-2 provided a $50.7 billion package of disaster assistance largely focused on responding to Hurricane Sandy. Additionally, Congress increased the National Flood Insurance Program's borrowing authority by $9.7 billion, from $20.725 billion to $30.425 billion (P.L. 113-1, To temporarily increase the borrowing authority of the Federal Emergency Management Agency for carrying out the National Flood Insurance Program). Both of these supplemental relief laws are discussed separately in CRS Report R42869, *FY2013 Supplemental Funding for Disaster Relief.*

This report examines the potential effect of the Sandy Recovery Improvement Act of 2013 on disaster assistance procedures and programs. Part of the legislative intent of the Sandy Recovery Improvement Act of 2013 is to streamline administrative procedures and improve the effectiveness of several disaster assistance programs authorized by the Stafford Act, namely the Public Assistance Program, the Individual Assistance Program, and the Hazard Mitigation Grant Program.[2] The law reforms the Stafford Act in part by reauthorizing several "pilot" programs established previously in Title VI of P.L. 109-295, the Post-Katrina Emergency Management Reform Act of 2006 (PKEMRA).[3] P.L. 113-2 also authorizes tribes to request a declaration of an emergency or major disaster, as was previously only allowed for states. It also directs FEMA to establish procedures for arbitrating disputes relating to disaster assistance, and directs FEMA to create a national strategy for mitigating the cost of future disasters. In the context of overall supplemental funding for disaster relief being debated by the Congress, the disaster assistance programs modified by the law are funded by the Disaster Relief Fund (DRF).[4] More detailed explanations of the modifications enacted by the law are provided below.

---

[1] The Stafford Act is codified at 42 U.S.C. §5121 et seq.

[2] See a discussion of the purpose of the law in the consideration of the originating bill, H.R. 219, "Sandy Recovery Improvement Act of 2013," House debate, *Congressional Record*, daily edition, January 14, 2013, pp. H65-72.

[3] 6 U.S.C. §701 et seq.

[4] For more the DRF, see CRS Report R40708, *Disaster Relief Funding and Emergency Supplemental Appropriations*, by Bruce R. Lindsay and Justin Murray.

Legislative History

On December 28, 2012, near the end of the 112th Congress, the Senate approved H.R. 1, the Disaster Relief Appropriations Act, 2013. The bill would have provided $60.41 billion in supplemental appropriations for disaster assistance and mitigation, and included a suite of legislative provisions that included reforms to several disaster assistance authorities. Included within the bill was the Disaster Recovery Act of 2012 (provided as a general provision, Section 609, to the Homeland Security title). No further action was taken on this bill during the 112th Congress.

On January 14, 2013, the House passed H.R. 219, the Sandy Recovery Improvement Act of 2013. This bill had many similarities to the Disaster Recovery Act of 2012, as passed by the Senate in the 112th Congress, including many provisions that were identical or very similar to each other. For more on these similarities, see the **Appendix**. Pursuant to the provisions of H.Res. 23, in the engrossment of H.R. 152, the Disaster Relief Appropriations Act, 2013, the text of H.R. 219 as passed by the House was added as new matter at the end of H.R. 152 (Division B—Sandy Recovery Improvement Act of 2013). H.R. 152 was passed by the House on January 15, 2013, and received by the Senate on January 22, 2013. The Senate passed H.R. 152 unchanged on January 28, 2013, and it was signed into law as P.L. 113-2 the next day.

Explanation of Provisions

The following sections of the report examine the effect of the Sandy Recovery Improvement Act of 2013 on disaster assistance procedures and programs. The provisions are not analyzed in numerical order, but rather consolidated by the program or policy subject affected by the provisions.

Tribal Requests for a Major Disaster or Emergency Declaration under the Stafford Act

Section 1110 of the Sandy Recovery Improvement Act of 2013 amends Sections 401 and 501 of the Stafford Act which contain the procedures for requesting types of disaster declarations.[5] Previously, tribal groups were treated as local governments and thus not permitted to directly request disaster declarations from the federal government. As with local governments, the tribes were dependent on a request being made by the governor of the state where their territory is located.[6]

Tribal governments argued that the previous provision in the Stafford Act undermined their independence and sovereignty. This change in declaration policy for tribal groups had been sought by FEMA to strengthen its government-to-government relationships with tribal groups and

---

[5] 42 U.S.C. §§5170 and 5191.

[6] Section 102 (7) defined local governments as including "an Indian tribe or authorized tribal organization, or Alaska Native village or organization." Section 401 of Stafford noted that "all requests shall be made by the Governor of the affected state."

improve emergency management in those areas.[7] As FEMA Administrator Craig Fugate stated in testimony before the Senate Indian Affairs Committee:

> The updated policy reiterates the Agency's view of tribal governments as inherently sovereign nations and not political subdivisions of states. To this end, and to the extent permitted by law, FEMA consults with tribal governments and addresses any concerns before taking actions that may affect those nations.
>
> In addition, the new policy expressly states that FEMA will identify and take reasonable, appropriate steps to eliminate or diminish procedural impediments to working directly and effectively with tribal governments. In particular, the policy states that FEMA will review portions of the Robert T. Stafford Disaster Relief and Emergency Assistance Act, and other laws, policies, and administrative rules in emergency management activities to determine how FEMA may work more directly with local tribal communities.[8]

Currently, the Stafford Act includes "an Indian tribe or authorized tribal organization, or Alaska Native village or organization" in the definition of local governments.[9] With this amendment, tribes are also now equivalent to states in their ability to request a major disaster declaration or an emergency declaration from the President.

Tribes had sought this authority for various reasons. While tribes and Native Americans have long received assistance under Stafford Act declarations, working through the state government for all assistance has been viewed as an issue of tribal sovereignty. States might at times be reluctant to request on behalf of a tribe when the damage was localized on tribal property. Other challenges to administering disaster relief involved language barriers and the physical isolation of some tribal lands.[10] Also the tribes wished to have the same ability as states to help manage the response and recovery from a disaster. All of these factors created challenges for emergency management following disaster events in tribal areas.

Under this amendment, the "Chief Executive of an Indian Tribal Government" is able to submit a request for a declaration by the President. In addition, the "Savings provision" of this section ensures that a tribal government is not prohibited from receiving assistance under a declaration made by the President at the request of the governor, if the President has not made a separate declaration for the tribal government. In effect, a tribal government will retain the ability to be treated as a local government in those situations.

Cost Share Adjustments for Indian Tribal Governments

Section 1110 also includes a cost-share adjustment for tribal governments. Under current law, states must provide up to 25% of certain disaster costs, with some adjustments possible under

---

[7] Rob Capriccioso, "FEMA Wants Tribes to be Equal to States," *Indian Country Today Media Network,* December 7, 2011, at http://indiancountrytodaymedianetwork.com/article/fema-wants-tribes-to-be-equal-to-states-66244.

[8] Testimony of FEMA Administrator Craig Fugate, in U.S. Congress, Senate Committee on Indian Affairs, *Facing Floods and Fires—Emergency Preparedness for Natural Disasters in Native Communities,* 112th Congress, 1st. Sess., July 31, 2011.

[9] 42 U.S.C. §5122.

[10] For an example of these difficulties, see DHS/FEMA Region VIII—"A disaster on the reservation," at http://www.clintonlibrary.gov/assets/storage/Research%20-%20Digital%20Library/ClintonAdminHistoryProject/21-30/Box%2025/1229761-fema-regions-3.pdf.

regulatory guidelines.[11] Section 1110 of P.L. 113-2 adds a new Section 401(c)(1) to the Stafford Act which permits the President to:

> waive or adjust any payment of a non-federal contribution with respect to the assistance if –
>
> (A) the President has the authority to waive or adjust the payment under another provision of this Act; and
>
> (B) the President determines that the waiver or adjustment is necessary and appropriate.

The degree of flexibility that is available for the President to set the cost-share for a tribal government is dependent upon the type of assistance being provided. For example, this new Section 401(c)(1)(A) of the Stafford Act appears to retain the cost-share under Section 404 for the Hazard Mitigation Grant Program which states that the President may contribute "up to 75 percent of the cost of hazard mitigation measures."[12] However, the President may have greater discretion under this provision to waive cost-shares for tribal governments for the Public Assistance (Section 406) program which, by FEMA regulation, adjusts to a 90% federal, 10% state and local cost share.[13] As with Section 206 of the Stafford Act, the President is charged with establishing the criteria for such adjustments.

Changes to the Individual Assistance Program

Individual Assistance Factors

FEMA's past judgments involving the Individual Assistance program and the declaration process have provoked interest in the factors FEMA considers when deciding whether to provide Individual Assistance during disasters and how those factors are interpreted. Since it helps determine the extent of federal supplemental assistance, both Congress and state governments share an interest in the declaration policy. Section 1109 of the Sandy Recovery Improvement Act of 2013 calls for FEMA to review its existing regulations that set forth the factors it considers when deciding whether to provide Individual Assistance during disasters (44 C.F.R. §206.48). This review is required within one year of enactment (which is January 29, 2014).

One significant argument for mandating such a review of Individual Assistance factors is that these factors have not been adjusted since they first appeared in regulation in 1999. FEMA is to undertake this review in cooperation with representatives of state, tribal, and local emergency management agencies. The intent of the section is to speed up the declaration process through this review. The current factors that FEMA considers when considering a declaration or a designation within a declaration are listed in its regulations.[14] No special weight is assigned to any of the six factors as they are listed in the regulations.[15] This provision directs that FEMA give special

---

[11] For information regarding current cost-share regulations, see 44 C.F.R. §206.47.

[12] 42 U.S.C. §5170c.

[13] For further discussion on cost-shares see CRS Report R41101, *FEMA Disaster Cost-Shares: Evolution and Analysis*, by Francis X. McCarthy.

[14] 44 CFR §206.48(b).

[15] For further discussion of these factors, see CRS Report RL34146, *FEMA's Disaster Declaration Process: A Primer*, by Francis X. McCarthy.

attention to the second factor listed, trauma, when FEMA is measuring the "severity, magnitude and impact of a disaster." Currently, the regulation defines trauma as follows:

> We consider the degree of trauma to a state and to communities. Some of the conditions that might cause trauma are:
>
> (i) Large numbers of injuries and deaths;
>
> (ii) Large scale disruption of normal community functions and services; and
>
> (iii) Emergency needs such as extended or widespread loss of power or water.[16]

Each of the existing factors considered for an IA declaration can be important in the decision-making process but the reference to the "extended or widespread loss of power" in the trauma factor section speaks to recent experiences in many states and wide-spread frustrations during disaster situations. Those frustrations are exacerbated during long power outages and perceived delays in assessing the impact of a disaster.

Child Care

Section 1108(a) of the Sandy Recovery Improvement Act of 2013 also impacts the Individual Assistance program by amending Section 408 of the Stafford Act. Since Hurricane Katrina, a great deal of attention has been given to the plight of children during natural disaster events. One of the areas under consideration has been how to provide child care assistance during especially trying circumstances. One of the challenges is that many such providers of these services are private entities and the Stafford Act assists only government and non-profit organizations. As the Commission on Children and Disasters noted:

> Expanding federal grant eligibility may be justified because many of the services provided by private entities such as child care facilities and physical and mental health clinics provide a service that fills a gap left by limited local, state, and federal resources.[17]

In approaching how to address the identified needs, Section 1108(a) includes "child care" as an eligible expense under the Other Needs Assistance (ONA) program. ONA is part of Section 408 of the Stafford Act, the Federal Assistance to Individuals and Households Program (IHP).[18] IHP is best known as the authority for FEMA's temporary housing program but ONA is also an important part of the program that attempts to address immediate needs that are not met by insurance or other means.

ONA is emergency assistance that helps a family or individual address immediate needs. The provision adds "child care" to a list of eligible activities that currently includes medical, dental and funeral expenses. ONA can also include replacement of personal property (such as clothing and furniture), transportation costs, and other expenses deemed necessary for recovery.

---

[16] 44 CFR §206.48(b)(2).

[17] For additional information, see CRS Report R41080, *The National Commission on Children and Disasters: Overview and Issues*, by Natalie Keegan.

[18] 42 U.S.C. §5174.

While the federal government pays all housing costs, expenses under ONA are cost-shared with the state on a 75% federal, 25% state basis. IHP assistance, that is, temporary housing and ONA, is limited to 18 months and total assistance of $31,900 per household.[19]

Federal Assistance to Individuals and Households

Pilot Program Made Permanent

Section 1103 of the Sandy Recovery Improvement Act of 2013 would make permanent a pilot program initiated by PKEMRA (P.L. 109-295).

> The Individuals and Households Pilot Program authorizes the President, through the FEMA Administrator, to increase the use of existing rental housing to provide temporary housing for victims of major disasters. Through the pilot program, which expires December 31, 2008, the Administrator is to provide for the repair and improvement of multi-family rental properties in disaster areas to increase the rental stock available to disaster victims in the immediate area. The FEMA Administrator may enter into lease agreements with the owners of multi-family units to achieve FEMA's housing goals, with specified restrictions.[20]

As noted previously, the Individuals and Households Program (IHP) consists of temporary housing and the Other Needs Assistance (ONA) program. Section 1103 increases FEMA's options for providing temporary housing under IHP.

It could be argued that the authority to take this approach already existed broadly in the Stafford Act in the section specifying "direct assistance" that mentions the authority to provide temporary housing units "by purchase or lease."[21] However, since that authority has only been used previously for the purchase of manufactured housing, the specific authority established by Section 1103 may be helpful to the recovery process in providing additional options for temporary housing. Given the work necessary to refurbish units, this form of housing may also contribute to the local economy in the disaster-affected area.

Lease and Repair of Rental Units for Temporary Housing

Section 1103 also authorizes FEMA to enter into lease agreements with private owners of multi-unit apartment facilities. The agreement would include the government paying for repairs or improvements to these apartment units to make them habitable. In return, the owners would agree to lease the improved apartments to house eligible disaster victims. The costs of the repairs would be deducted from the total amount of the lease agreement.

---

[19] Department of Homeland Security, Federal Emergency Management Agency, "Notice of Maximum Amount of Assistance Under the Individuals and Households Program," 77 *Federal Register*, pp. 61425-61426, October 9, 2012, at https://Federalregister.gov/a/201.-24675.

[20] CRS Report RL33729, *Federal Emergency Management Policy Changes After Hurricane Katrina: A Summary of Statutory Provisions*, coordinated by Keith Bea.

[21] 42 U.S.C. §5174(1)(B)(i).

Pilot Program Experience

There was a limited piloting of this multi-family rental unit project in Texas following Hurricane Ike and in Iowa after flooding. FEMA's report to Congress noted:

> The total estimated cost for the Iowa project is $76,854. The estimated cost of providing seven manufactured homes for an equal period of time is $439,376. The total estimated savings to the federal government is $363,522, or 83% less than the cost of providing manufactured homes. The total estimated cost for the Texas pilot project is $897,358. The estimated cost to provide 32 manufactured homes for an equal period of time is $2,650,624. The total estimated savings to the federal government is $1,753,266, or 66% less than the cost of providing manufactured homes.[22]

Although FEMA reported favorable results from the pilot program, this may be an option of limited utility depending on the area where the disaster occurs and the availability of undamaged or unrented units. On the other hand, this arguably provides FEMA with another tool for helping to house individuals in their home area while also making expenditures in that same area that can contribute to the overall recovery.

Changes to the Public Assistance Program

Public Assistance Alternative Procedures

In brief, the PA Program helps state and local governments, as well as certain eligible private non-profits, in their response and recovery to a disaster by providing financial assistance in the form of grants to clear debris and repair and rebuild facilities. Following past disasters, most notably Hurricane Katrina, the PA program has been criticized for being cumbersome and too inflexible to address the needs of local governments and communities. These criticisms were highlighted in several hearings in the immediate aftermath of Hurricane Sandy.[23]

Section 1102 of the Sandy Recovery Improvement Act of 2013 revises the Stafford Act by creating a new Section 428 that authorizes the Administrator to establish and adopt alternative procedures for administering federal assistance under the Public Assistance program.[24] The alternative procedures apply to all traditional categories of Public Assistance (PA) except for Category B—Emergency Protective Measures.[25]

---

[22] U.S. Department of Homeland Security, Federal Emergency Management Agency, *Individuals and Households Pilot Program, Fiscal Year 2009 Report to Congress*, May 19, 2009, p. 4.

[23] Most notably, see the testimony of Mark Riley, the Deputy Director of the Governor's Office of Homeland Security and Emergency Preparedness for the State of Louisiana in U.S. Congress, House Committee on Transportation and Infrastructure, *Review of the Preparedness Response and Recovery from Hurricane*, 112th Cong., 2nd sess., December 4, 2012 (official transcript not yet available).

[24] The Public Assistance program is authorized by Sections 403(a)(3)(A), 406, 407, and 502(a)(5) of the Stafford Act. Respectively these sections of the Stafford Act refer to emergency debris removal; repair, restoration, and replacement of damaged facilities; non-essential debris removal; and debris removal (via an emergency declaration).

[25] The eligibility of costs in Category B assistance would be revised in Section 1108(a) of the Sandy Recovery Improvement Act of 2013. Under FEMA policy guidance for PA, there are seven categories. Under "emergency work" there is Category A—Debris Removal and Category B—Emergency Protective Measures, and under "permanent work" there is Category C—Roads and Bridges, Category D—Water Control Facilities, Category E—Buildings and Equipment, Category F—Utilities, and Category G—Parks, Recreational Facilities, and Other Items. These categories (continued...)

The stated goals of the new alternative procedure are to reduce the cost of federal government assistance; increase the administrative flexibility of the PA program; expedite the process of providing and using the assistance; and create incentives for applicants to complete projects in a timely and cost-effective manner.[26] The provision does not *require* the Administrator to adopt and develop such procedures[27] nor would the Administrator be obligated to approve projects under the alternative procedures.[28] Any participation in the adopted alternative procedures is voluntary at the request of the applicant.[29]

The law also mandates several requirements for the alternative procedures.[30] These requirements can be split into two elements; those changes that apply to the repair, restoration, and replacement of damaged facilities under Section 406 of the Stafford Act, and those changes that apply to debris removal assistance under Sections 403(a)(3)(A), 407, and 502(a)(5) of the Stafford Act.[31] For the applicability of the overall alternative procedures prospectively and retrospectively to major disasters, see the "Applicability to Prior Declared Disasters" section in this report.

Alternative Procedures for Section 406 of the Stafford Act

The alternative procedures include three major revisions for how FEMA can provide assistance for the repair, restoration, and replacement of damaged facilities[32] (assistance provided through Section 406 of the Stafford Act). The provision will allow for procedures to issue grants to recipients based on estimates of their eligible cost as opposed to reimbursement for eligible actual costs; procedures revising the in-lieu contribution authorized in Section 406(c) of the Stafford Act; and procedures for consolidating project worksheets for public assistance projects. Each revision is examined in full below.

Grants Based on Estimates of Eligible Costs

Under the new alternative procedures, FEMA is authorized to issue public assistance grants to applicants based on estimates of their total public assistance eligibility. Of note, the authority to provide grants based on estimates of eligible assistance already existed in Section 406(e) of the

---

(...continued)

are defined in Federal Emergency Management Agency, *Public Assistance Guide*, FEMA 322, 2007, at http://www.fema.gov/public-assistance-policy-and-guidance.

[26] See 127 Stat. 40 and the new §428(c) of the Stafford Act and its subparts.

[27] See 127 Stat. 40 and the new §428(b) of the Stafford Act, and that it states the Administrator "may" adopt alternative procedures in coordination with state, tribal, and local governments, and owners or operators of private nonprofit facilities. This is distinction is important, as in past legislative changes to the Stafford Act the President and/or the Administrator have not always implemented some of the options afforded to them in law.

[28] See 127 Stat. 39 and the new §428(a) of the Stafford Act, which states that the Administrator "may" approve projects.

[29] See 127 Stat. 40 and the new §428(d) of the Stafford Act. Voluntary participation is subject to "procedures determined by the Administrator." It is unclear if an applicant would be able to choose to participate in the alternative procedures project by project, or if the Administrator may require the applicant to use the procedures for one set of projects or for the whole disaster declaration.

[30] See 127 Stat. 40 and the new §428(e) and its subparts of the Stafford Act.

[31] See 127 Stat. 40-41 and the new §428(e)(1) and §428(e)(2) of the Stafford Act, respectively.

[32] There are two types of facilities eligible for assistance: public facilities, which are owned by state or local governments, and private non-profit facilities that provide critical services. These terms are defined in full in Section 102(9) and (10) of the Stafford Act.

Stafford Act. This authority for issuing grants based on estimates was added to the Stafford Act by Section 205(d) of the Disaster Mitigation Act of 2000 (P.L. 106-390).[33] In that law, the President was directed by Section 406(e)(3) to convene an expert panel on how costs should be estimated by FEMA, and to issue regulations implementing these cost estimation procedures. Although the expert panel convened and issued a report,[34] the regulations implementing the statute have not been issued.[35] In addition, Section 689j of PKEMRA authorized the creation of a Public Assistance Pilot Program[36] which, in part, similarly allowed the President to issue grants based on estimates.

Despite previously having the authority to issue grants based on estimates, in most situations FEMA reimburses public assistance applicants on an "actual cost" basis instead of using estimates. Therefore, FEMA generally provides the full assistance amount only after the eligible work on a public assistance project has been completed.[37] FEMA does frequently use a cost-estimating process (called the Cost Estimating Format by FEMA) for some PA projects to help anticipate the end obligation for the project. This enables FEMA to anticipate future costs and outlays for PA projects. However, as a general practice, FEMA only issues grants based on those estimates for PA projects when:

- A project is estimated to cost less than $67,500, and therefore is eligible for simplified procedures as authorized in Section 422 of the Stafford Act;[38]

- An applicant in a project is deciding to receive an in-lieu contribution through Section 406(c) of the Stafford Act (an "alternate project"[39] in FEMA terminology); and

- Significant improvements are being planned for the facility (an "improved project"[40] in FEMA terminology).[41]

---

[33] 114 Stat. 1564. Likewise, Section 689j of the Department of Homeland Security Appropriations Act, 2007 (P.L. 109-295) authorized the creation of a Public Assistance Pilot Program (PA Pilot Program) which, in part, also allowed the President to issue grants based on estimates of eligible cost. For more on the PA Pilot program, see Federal Emergency Management Agency, *Public Assistance Pilot Program: Program Guidance*, June 2007, at http://www.fema.gov/pdf/about/regions/regioniii/papilot.pdf.; and see Federal Emergency Management Agency, *Public Assistance Pilot Program: Fiscal Year 2009 Report to Congress*, May 20, 2009, at http://www.fema.gov/library/viewRecord.do?id=3683.

[34] Federal Emergency Management Agency, *Public Assistance: Expert Panel on Cost Estimating*, Recommendation Report of Federal Advisory Committee 10733, October 2002, at http://coop.fema.gov/pdf/government/grant/pa/cefrep.pdf.

[35] Recent proposed bills, such as Section 209 of the FEMA Reauthorization Act of 2012 (H.R. 2903, as passed by the House), have called for the President to issue these regulations within 180 days of enactment.

[36] 120 Stat. 1455. For more on the PA Pilot program, see Federal Emergency Management Agency, *Public Assistance Pilot Program: Program Guidance*, June 2007, at http://www.fema.gov/pdf/about/regions/regioniii/papilot.pdf; and Federal Emergency Management Agency, *Public Assistance Pilot Program: Fiscal Year 2009 Report to Congress*, May 20, 2009, at http://www.fema.gov/library/viewRecord.do?id=3683.

[37] FEMA will, under some circumstances, provide advances on assistance funds (see 44 C.F.R. §13.21). For regulations guiding how FEMA currently provides assistance for Section 406 of the Stafford Act, see 44 C.F.R. §206.200-339.

[38] For more on this authority, see the section "Simplified Procedures" of this report.

[39] For more on what FEMA calls an "alternate project," see an explanation at Federal Emergency Management Agency, *Alternative Project*, at.http://www.fema.gov/public-assistance-project-formulation-cost-estimating/alternate-project.

[40] For more on what FEMA calls an "improved project," see an explanation at Federal Emergency Management Agency, *Improved Project*, at http://www.fema.gov/public-assistance-project-formulation-cost-estimating/improved-project.

The authority to issue grants based on estimates of eligible costs will be part of the alternative procedures an applicant can elect to use for PA projects.[42] One important policy issue remains unclear in the law, and will be left to FEMA to interpret in their establishment and implementation of the procedures. The Sandy Recovery Improvement Act does not indicate if the grants are available for any amount of assistance (in terms of dollars), or if the grant assistance will be limited at some dollar amount. The PA Pilot Program authorized by PKEMRA had similarly worded language on grants based on estimates. When FEMA interpreted this similar authority, they implemented procedures that only gave estimated assistance on single facility projects up to $500,000.[43] Therefore, in implementation of these alternative procedures, FEMA may only allow grants based on estimates up to a certain dollar amount. Limiting the availability of grants based on estimates to under a set amount might contradict the legislative intent of this provision, but appears to be a conceivable option given the language and past FEMA precedent.

The Sandy Recovery Improvement Act of 2013 also provides guidance on how estimates could be developed by FEMA. As discussed previously, regulations implementing cost estimation procedures under Section 406(e)(3) of the Stafford Act have not been issued. In absence of such regulations, the alternative procedures include basic guidelines for determining the estimated eligible assistance of each project(s). First, FEMA should, at the applicant's request, accept the estimates of professionally licensed engineers, so long as the estimate complies with FEMA regulations, policy, and guidance.[44] No definition or guidance is provided for what constitutes a "professionally licensed engineer," therefore it will be up to the Administrator to determine what qualifications are required to be professionally licensed. Second, in instances where the estimated cost is over $5 million, the applicant is allowed to request an independent expert panel to review and validate the cost estimate.[45] No further guidance is provided on the composition of the independent expert panel, or the authority this panel has to revise or amend estimated costs. Therefore, these factors will be developed in FEMA's implementation of the procedure.

The law also provides guidance on what will occur in instances where the estimated grant amount does not equal the final actual costs of the applicant's project(s).[46] In instances where the amount provided by grant is less than the actual eligible cost, the applicant will have to agree to pay the overages.[47] In instances where the grant is more than the actual eligible cost of the project(s), FEMA has the authority to allow the applicant to use the extra funds for mitigation activities or other activities improving future disaster relief.[48] It remains unclear what will become of the excess funds if they are not used by the applicant for such prescribed activities. Unlike the cost-

---

(...continued)

[41] For more on how and when FEMA currently uses their Cost-Estimating Format, see an explanation at Federal Emergency Management Agency, *Public Assistance: Cost Estimating Format Standard Operating Procedure*, at http://www.fema.gov/public-assistance-cost-estimating-format-standard-operating-procedure.

[42] See 127 Stat. 40-41 and the new §§428(e)(1) and (2) of the Stafford Act.

[43] See Federal Emergency Management Agency, *Public Assistance Pilot Program: Fiscal Year 2009 Report to Congress*, May 20, 2009.

[44] See 127 Stat. 41 and the new §428(e)(1)(F) of the Stafford Act.

[45] See 127 Stat. 40 and the new §428(e)(1)(E) of the Stafford Act.

[46] In other words, what will happen if FEMA grants more or less assistance based on an estimate than the applicant was ultimately eligible for once the true costs of a project(s) was revealed after completion—often many years later.

[47] See 127 Stat. 40 and the new §428(e)(1)(A) of the Stafford Act.

[48] See 127 Stat. 40 and the new §428(e)(1)(D)(i) and (ii) of the Stafford Act. It is likely that FEMA will issue guidance on the use of excess funds.

estimating procedures called for by Section 406(e)(2)(A) and (B) of the Stafford Act,[49] the guidelines laid out in this section do not include mention of a floor or ceiling percentage by which the actual cost of a project could come in under or over the estimate. In other words, there is no margin of error for the estimate to be different from actual cost.[50]

Some may argue that without an allowance for floor and ceiling percentages (the margin of error), the process of arriving at an acceptable cost estimate in these alternative procedures may be contentious, especially since it is to the applicant's benefit to ensure that the cost estimate is equal to or higher than the ultimate actual costs of the project. The applicant may be incentivized to seek a high estimate because if actual costs come in lower than the estimate, they are able to use the additional funds for other purposes and are also able to avoid having to pay for unaccounted costs without federal assistance (as would be the case if the estimate were too low).

In-Lieu Contribution

Under pre-existing authorities provided in Section 406 of the Stafford Act, state and local governments, as well as owner/operators of eligible private non-profits, may elect to receive an "in-lieu contribution" of federal assistance for PA projects. In brief, applicants can request that FEMA provide, by grant, the amount of assistance that would have normally been provided for the repair, restoration, or replacement of the current facility. This in-lieu contribution/grant can be used to repair or build an alternate facility or for mitigation measures.[51] In Section 406, such a decision by an applicant needs to be in the interest of the public welfare as determined by the applicant. However, FEMA is obligated by law to reduce the amount of assistance provided "in lieu" to the applicant. For public facilities, the reduction is 10% of the eligible cost for repairing the existing facility, for private non-profit facilities, the reduction is 25%.[52] FEMA applies the reduction to the estimated eligible cost of repairing the current facility, *not* the estimated costs of new project or mitigation activities.[53] This penalty on the in-lieu contribution has been considered a deterrent to applicants from recovering the facilities in innovative ways as opposed to rebuilding and repairing the facility back to the way it was prior to the disaster.

In the alternative procedures established by the Sandy Recovery Improvement Act of 2013, the in-lieu contributions will not be reduced by 10% for public facilities or 25% for private non-profit

---

[49] 42 U.S.C. §5172.

[50] In the expert panel recommendations created after DMA 2000, the panel determined that an error range of 10% was appropriate to serve as the "floor" and "ceiling" percentage called for in Stafford Act. This means that had FEMA implemented the regulations required by Section 406(e)(3)(C) of the Stafford Act, there would be some flexibility in how situations where the actual cost of was different than the estimated cost of assistance, as described in Section 406(e)(2) of the Stafford Act.

[51] Section 406(c)(1)(B) of the Stafford Act authorizes applicants to use in-lieu contributions to repair other facilities, build new facilities, or to provide hazard mitigation at other sites. For example, if an elementary school was substantially destroyed after a disaster, the local government may decide that instead of rebuilding that particular school (and having FEMA reimburse them for the federal share of the eligible cost of doing so), the community may be better served by using that money to build a new high school or to better protect a nearby police station (perhaps because of shifting demographic needs in their population).

[52] See §406(c)(1)(A) of the Stafford Act for public facilities, and §406(c)(2)(A) for private non-profit facilities. Federal assistance for public facility alternate projects was raised from 75% of the eligible federal share to 90% of the federal share in Section 609 of the Security and Accountability For Every Port Act of 2006 (SAFE Port Act, P.L. 109-347).

[53] Returning to prior example in footnote 51, this means FEMA provides 90% of what they estimated to be the total eligible federal assistance for repairing the original damaged elementary school, *not* 90% of the new eligible costs of building a different high school or mitigating future damages to the police station.

---

facilities.[54] In addition, the alternative procedures do not mention the Section 406 requirement that in-lieu contribution be in the interest of the public welfare, though such requirements may be added by FEMA in their implementation of this option to the alternative procedures.[55]

Consolidating Projects

Finally, the alternative procedures for repair and reconstruction projects will explicitly allow applicants to consolidate multiple individual facilities into a single project. Generally, this policy has previously been used to ease the administrative management of making repairs to multiple similar function facilities—such as all damaged elementary schools—by allowing them to be considered a single project. Using a grant estimating procedure, this could allow a local government, for instance, to receive a grant based on the estimate of damages to nine elementary schools, and use that money to build seven bigger elementary schools instead. However, the law does not specifically require facilities to be of a similar function, so hypothetically a local government could seek to combine a police station project with an elementary school project. How liberally projects could be consolidated remains unknown since the ability to consolidate projects is limited "to the extent determined appropriate by the Administrator."[56]

Alternative Procedures for Debris Removal Assistance

The new Section 428(e)(2) of the Stafford Act applies to debris removal assistance authorized by Sections 403(a)(3)(A), 407, and 502(a)(5) of the Stafford Act. This new section of the Stafford Act reauthorizes similar authorities to those granted by the PA Pilot Program established by PKEMRA. The alternative procedures authorities on debris removal allow the Administrator to:

- Provide grants on the basis of fixed estimates, in a similar fashion to the estimation procedures discussed previously for repair and reconstruction projects.

- Use a sliding scale for the federal share of debris removal based on the time it takes to finish debris removal that provides a federal larger share of the eligible cost to the applicant the quicker they complete the debris removal project, as a means of encourage faster work. For example, if a project is completed within 60 days, the federal government might pay 80% of the eligible cost, but if it is completed in 30 days, it might pay 90% of the cost.

- Allow applicants to recycle debris and use the proceeds from such recycling without reducing the award amount to encourage communities to reap financial and environmental benefits from recycling debris to the greatest extent possible.

---

[54] See 127 Stat. 40 and the new §428(e)(1)(c) of the Stafford Act.

[55] In the PA Pilot Program, FEMA was authorized to implement an in-lieu procedure that would have maintained the 90% assistance level for public facilities but did not mention a public welfare component. However, they did not exercise this authority, so it is unclear what impact, if any, the possible exclusion of the public welfare requirement would have for the program. In current law, the "public welfare" determination is made by the applicant (either a state/local government or an owner/operator of an eligible private non-profit), so FEMA does not have set regulations or policies on how this determination must be made. For more on why FEMA chose not to implement the in-lieu contribution policy in the PA Pilot Project, see Federal Emergency Management Agency, *Public Assistance Pilot Program: Fiscal Year 2009 Report to Congress*, May 20, 2009.

[56] As in, subject to FEMA regulations and guidance. See the new §428(e)(1)(C)) of the Stafford Act.

- Reimburse state, tribal, and local governments or owner/operators of private non-profits for the base and overtime wages of employees that are performing or administering debris removal projects.[57] In an immediate final rule issued on November 9, 2012, FEMA implemented a similar reimbursement policy for declarations made because of Hurricane Sandy.[58] This provision implements that policy in the alternative procedures permanently, for all future disasters (not just Hurricane Sandy).

- Provide financial incentives for governments with a FEMA-approved debris removal plan and one or more pre-qualified debris removal contracts prior to a disaster. In implementing this authority during the PA Pilot Program, FEMA offered an additional 5% federal share to applicants if they had the debris removal plan and two pre-qualified debris removal contracts in place.

During the PA Pilot Program, FEMA implemented some form of each of these authorities except that they chose *not* to implement a sliding scale, as they determined the policy may have been too complex to implement and would not have produced a financial savings.[59] In the findings reported by FEMA at the conclusion of the PA Pilot Program, FEMA generally saw positive results from the recycling of debris, financial incentives for debris planning, and reimbursement of wages policies. The positive results from the financial incentives and reimbursement of wage policies were confirmed in an audit conducted by the Inspector General of the Department of Homeland Security.[60] However, FEMA indicated that too few applicants used the grant estimating procedure to determine what impact, if any, it would have had on the efficacy of the assistance.[61]

Report Requirement

Section 1102 of the Sandy Recovery Improvement Act of 2013 requires the Inspector General of the Department of Homeland Security to assess the effectiveness of the alternative procedures for Section 406 of the Stafford Act.[62] The report will contain recommendations from the Inspector General about whether the procedures should be altered or continued in future legislation. Of note, this report is *not* required to assess the portion of the alternative procedures for debris removal assistance authorized by Sections 403(a)(3)(A), 407, and 502(a)(5) of the Stafford Act. The report will be issued in three to five years following the enactment of the alternative procedures and will be provided to the committees of jurisdiction for the Stafford Act. The

---

[57] Reimbursement of wages would be similar to the new authorities provided for emergency protective measures, with the noted exception that for debris removal no distinction is made between the types of government employee, and that the assistance is also available to private non-profit owners. For more on this issue, see the section "Essential Assistance" of this report.

[58] See Department of Homeland Security, "Debris Removal: Eligibility of Force Account Labor Straight-Time Costs under the Public Assistance Program for Hurricane Sandy," 77 *Federal Register* 67285, November 9, 2012.

[59] Federal Emergency Management Agency, *Public Assistance Pilot Program: Fiscal Year 2009 Report to Congress*, May 20, 2009.

[60] Department of Homeland Security, Office of Inspector General, *FEMA's Oversight and Management of Debris Removal Operations*, OIG-11-40, Washington, DC, February 2011, at http://www.oig.dhs.gov/assets/Mgmt/OIG_11-40_Feb11.pdf.

[61] Ibid.

[62] This report requirement is found in the new §428(g) of the Stafford Act. This report requirement was unique to the PA Alternative Procedures provision as passed in P.L. 113-2. It is not found in Section 609(c) of the Disaster Recovery Act of 2012.

issuance of the report may provide Congress with direction on how it could further revise the Stafford Act to improve the PA program.

Simplified Procedures

Section 422 of the Stafford Act authorizes FEMA to provide PA grants based on federal estimates of eligible costs, as opposed to reimbursing on eligible actual costs.[63] Providing this assistance via a federal estimate is deemed a "simplified procedure." Current law caps the availability of this simplified procedure to projects less than $67,500 for disasters declared after October 1, 2012. The cap is adjusted annually.[64] Projects under this ceiling are often referred to by FEMA as "small projects."

Section 1107 of the Sandy Recovery Improvement Act of 2013 revises Section 422 by requiring the Administrator to analyze whether it would be appropriate to raise the ceiling on small projects, based on a number of considerations including how the threshold impacts "cost-effectiveness, speed of recovery, capacity of grantees, past performance, and accountability measures."[65] The Administrator's findings will be provided in a report to the appropriate committees of Congress no later than one year after enactment (which is January 29, 2014). Following submission of this report, the President is instructed to direct the Administrator to establish a new ceiling for small project eligibility in the appropriate amount. This new threshold would be adjusted annually by the CPI and reviewed and re-established no later than every three years. Therefore, the analysis conducted by the Administrator could result in a new ceiling for simplified procedures being established within a year of enactment and every three years after.[66]

Essential Assistance

Section 1108(b) of the Sandy Recovery Improvement Act of 2013 revises Section 403 of the Stafford Act. Among other items, Section 403 of the Stafford Act authorizes the President and federal agencies to provide assistance for essential services.[67] As listed in the statute, essential assistance includes activities like debris removal, the provision of temporary facilities for schools and other essential community services, and public warning about future risks and hazards.[68] In addition to performing the essential activities themselves in support of communities, federal

---

[63] 42 U.S.C. §5189. Specifically, eligible costs under Section 403, 406, 407, or 502 of the Stafford Act. For more on how grants are issued by estimate, see the "Alternative Procedures for Section 406 of the Stafford Act" section of the report.

[64] The statute set the ceiling at $35,000, adjusted annually according to the Consumer Price Index for All Urban Customers. This figure is now adjusted to $67,500 for all disasters declared on or after October 1, 2012, see Federal Emergency Management Agency, "Notice of Adjustment of Disaster Grant," 77 *Federal Register* 61423, October 9, 2012.

[65] 127 Stat. 46 and the new §422(b)(1)(A) of the Stafford Act.

[66] Though the law indicates that the President shall determine if an increase in the threshold is appropriate (see the new §422(b)(1)(A) of the Stafford Act), the Administrator is instructed to establish the threshold at "an appropriate amount" in §422(b)(2)(A) of the Stafford Act. Conceivably, this amount may not be higher than the previous threshold, if the President and Administrator have determined within reason that the same or lower threshold is appropriate.

[67] Section 403 authorizes many forms of assistance that federal agencies, upon the direction of the President, may provide to address "the immediate threats to life and property resulting from a major disaster" (42 U.S.C. §5170b). Further, federal agencies are authorized to perform work on public or private property that is "essential to saving lives and protecting and preserving property or public health and safety" (§403(a)(3) of the Stafford Act).

[68] See §403(a)(3) of the Stafford Act for a full list of the activities included specifically in the law.

---

agencies are authorized to make contributions to state or local governments, or operators of private nonprofit facilities who are providing such essential assistance at a federal share of no less than 75%.[69]

Generally, FEMA refers to such activities eligible under Section 403 as "emergency work," which includes some forms of "debris removal" activities and all "emergency protective measures." FEMA has issued regulations guiding how the federal government will reimburse state and local governments for these activities.[70] Under regulations and policy directives, FEMA has determined that, in general, only the overtime wages of permanent employees working for the state and local governments are eligible for reimbursement (as in, *not* the base pay and benefits or "straight time" of an employee).[71] In contrast, FEMA has determined that the full cost of contract labor for this work is eligible for reimbursement.

In a revision of this previous FEMA policy, the Sandy Recovery Improvement Act of 2013 further specifies in Section 403 that the President may reimburse the base and overtime pay and benefits of permanent employees of state, tribal, and local governments for emergency protective measures. This assistance is limited to "work [that] is not typically performed by the employees" and to "the type of work [that] may otherwise be carried out by contract or agreement with private organizations, firms, or individuals."[72] Therefore, FEMA is authorized to reimburse both the base and overtime pay and benefits for some, but not all, permanent employees conducting emergency protective measures. This new provision does not impact the treatment of wages for private nonprofits and it would continue to allow the reimbursement of overtime and hazardous duty pay of all state and local permanent employees conducting emergency protective measures, consistent with past FEMA policy. Other sections of the Sandy Recovery Improvement Act of 2013 address the reimbursement of wages for debris removal.[73]

Under pre-existing FEMA procedures, some argued that state and local governments are encouraged not to use their own employees for emergency protective measures because contract work is currently fully eligible for reimbursement, while the base wages of state and local governments' employees are not reimbursable. The revisions made by this law for reimbursement may address these concerns over FEMA procedures. However, the new law authorizing reimbursement of base pay and benefits would only apply to the permanent employees of state and local governments who do not typically perform emergency protective measures.[74] Therefore,

---

[69] Section 403(a)(4) of the Stafford Act.

[70] See 44 C.F.R. §206.201(b) for the definition of emergency work, and primarily 44 C.F.R. §206.225 for regulations on emergency work. "Debris removal" is subcategory A and "Emergency protective measures" is subcategory B of the Public Assistance program. For a full list of activities FEMA considers eligible under each category, see Federal Emergency Management Agency, *Public Assistance Guide*, FEMA 322, 2007, at http://www.fema.gov/public-assistance-policy-and-guidance.

[71] See primarily 44 C.F.R. §206.228(a)(2) and Federal Emergency Management Agency, *Labor Costs—Emergency Work*, FEMA Recovery Policy RP9525.7, November 16, 2006, at http://www.fema.gov/pdf/government/grant/pa/9525_7.pdf. An exception to this standard is provided in 44 C.F.R. §206.202(f)(1)(ii), which allows for the reimbursement of the base salaries of a host-state's permanently employed staff who are supporting evacuations or shelters.

[72] See 127 Stat. 47 the new §§403(d)(1)(A)(i) and (ii) of the Stafford Act.

[73] As noted previously, "emergency protective measures" is a subcomponent of "emergency work" and does not include debris removal, which is a separate category of the PA program. See discussion of the reimbursement for debris removal in "Alternative Procedures for Debris Removal Assistance."

[74] See the clause "not typically performed by the employees" in the new §403(d)(1)(A)(i) of the Stafford Act.

---

following similar logic as before, state and local governments may still be encouraged not to use their employees who typically conduct emergency protective measures in favor of their employees who do not typically do that work, or to continue to contract for emergency protective measures. Therefore, many of the implications of this policy will depend on FEMA's interpretation of which state and local government employees "typically" conduct emergency protective measures and which do not, as well as what work "may otherwise be carried out by contract or agreement."[75]

Unified Federal Review[76]

Activities necessary to recover or rebuild a community in the wake of a disaster may be subject to various local, state, tribal, or federal laws intended to protect cultural, natural, or environmental resources (e.g., the National Historic Preservation Act, Endangered Species Act, or Clean Water Act). Section 1106 of the Sandy Recovery Improvement Act of 2013 revises the Stafford Act to create a new Section 429 and would require the President, in consultation with the Council on Environmental Quality (CEQ) and the Advisory Council on Historic Preservation, to establish a Unified Federal Review process to address potential delays related to federal compliance with requirements applicable to activities associated with disaster recovery projects. This review process is required to be established within 18 months of enactment. Most federal agencies currently have such procedures in place. Also, CEQ has provided guidance to federal agencies regarding procedures to expedite compliance with applicable environmental review requirements of the National Environmental Policy Act.[77]

Changes to the Hazard Mitigation Program

Section 1104 of the Sandy Recovery Improvement Act of 2013 amends Section 404 of the Stafford Act, which authorizes the Hazard Mitigation Grant Program (HMGP).[78]

Streamlined Procedures

This provision seeks to accelerate the implementation of HMGP assistance. The new Section 404(d)(2) of the Stafford Act requires the utilization of streamlined procedures in order to provide assistance more rapidly. The program has traditionally moved at a slower pace than other disaster assistance given its processes and the types of projects it funds. But the slower pace has troubled public officials in affected disaster areas.[79]

---

[75] See this clause in the new §403(d)(1)(A)(ii) of the Stafford Act.

[76] This section was prepared by Linda Luther, Analyst in Environmental Policy, 7-6852. For more information, see CRS Report RL34650, *Implementing the National Environmental Policy Act (NEPA) for Disaster Response, Recovery, and Mitigation Projects*, by Linda Luther.

[77] See May 12, 2012, Memorandum for Heads of Federal Departments and Agencies from Nancy Sutley, CEQ Chair, regarding "Emergencies and the National Environmental Policy Act," at http://ceq.hss.doe.gov/ceq_regulations/ Emergencies_and_NEPA_Memorandum_12May2010.pdf.

[78] 42 U.S.C. §5170c.

[79] Bruce Eggler, "New Orleans officials frustrated over slow payments from Hazard Mitigation Grant Program", NOLA.com/The Times Picayune, December 16, 2010, at http://www.nola.com/politics/index.ssf/2010/12/ new_orleans_officials_frustrat.html.

One of the streamlining procedures that will be utilized is to treat multiple structures, generally clusters of houses, as a group. This procedure has some precedent since the Section 404 buy-out program has purchased large swaths of housing in repetitively flooded areas.[80] While each transaction would involve a voluntary commitment on the part of a homeowner for their participation, the packaging of parcels together is a common practice in seeking to remove vulnerable properties and prevent repeat federal expenditures to an at-risk area.

However, the new Section 404(d)(2) of the Stafford Act also references the Prototype Programmatic Agreement of FEMA as a way of addressing cost-effectiveness and cost-share issues for the multiple structures that may be a part of an HMGP project. FEMA has submitted a draft of a "Prototype" to the Advisory Commission on Historic Preservation (ACHP) but has not yet reached an agreement on the document in accordance with ACHP regulations.[81] FEMA has entered into programmatic agreements with states using the "Prototype" as a basic framework for organizing its work on historic preservation. But the "Prototype" does not address cost-effectiveness and has no influence on any cost-share provisions within FEMA programs.

The streamlined procedures stated in the new provision also include the analysis of environmental impacts to historic properties, cost-effectiveness and fulfillment of cost-share requirements for hazard mitigation measures. It also emphasizes that "adequate resources" should be devoted to this effort. Since FEMA has flexibility in its administration of the Stafford Act that direction may be useful.

However, the areas addressed in this section may be challenging provisions to accelerate. For example, the cost-effectiveness requirement can require substantial research into local history, replacement costs, and potential savings. Also, the cost-share for mitigation within the Stafford Act is not as flexible as other parts of Stafford. For the mitigation cost-share, the Stafford Act states that: "The President may contribute up to 75 percent of the cost-share of hazard mitigation measures."[82] However, the expectation of accelerating the process is partly explained and addressed by another part of the provision which permits the President to advance "not more than 25 percent of the amount of estimated cost prior to eligible costs being incurred."[83] This would increase the initial costs of the front end of the disaster but could arguably also speed up a mitigation process that has appeared cumbersome during previous disasters.

State Administration of HMGP

This provision provides the Administrator the authority to waive notice and rulemaking procedures to expeditiously implement procedures for states to administer the HMGP program. Since states cost-share the program (providing 25% of program costs), and establish state-wide priorities for HMGP funding, it may be considered appropriate that they have the option of administering the program. In fact, that authority was first placed in the Disaster Mitigation Act

---

[80] *Innovative Floodplain Management, Full Mitigation Best Practice Story, Lenoir County, North Carolina,* at http://www.fema.gov/mitigationbp/bestPracticeDetail.do?mitssid=290.

[81] 36 C.F.R. §800.14(b)(4).

[82] 42 U.S.C. §5170c.

[83] See 127 Stat. 43 and the new §404(e) of the Stafford Act.

of 2000, P.L. 106-390 which established the authority for state management of HMGP.[84] The previous law also asked the President to establish criteria for that management.

Given this waiver authority in P.L. 113-2, it appears that the criteria have yet to be established.[85] So this provision provides the authority for a pilot program for state management of the HMGP program while the Administrator is establishing the criteria. The Stafford Act already notes the state's involvement in HMGP and provides the first direction as to what state criteria might contain. The state's authority to manage HMGP is noted in in Section 404(c). That authority has the minimum criteria listed such as a state's ability and the states own mitigation plan and its overall commitment to mitigation. The current regulations also provide a foundation for state management since the regulations do have the requirements for a state administrative plan for the HMGP program.[86]

Dispute Resolution Pilot Program

It is common during the administration of disaster assistance for disputes to arise regarding the eligibility of various costs or activities for reimbursement. When there is disagreement on the scope of work and the costs involved, public assistance applicants have the ability to appeal FEMA's decisions.[87] The appeal process has two tiers; the initial appeal goes to the FEMA Regional Administrator where the disaster occurred and the second appeal goes to FEMA headquarters for a decision.[88] Some critics have argued that the appeals process is time-consuming. Some have also suggested that, though timelines exist in the law and regulations,[89] they are not consistently applied. As the DHS Inspector General pointed out:

> FEMA does not consistently adhere to timeliness standards governing the amount of time its officials have to provide determinations on appeals. We reviewed appeals that showed, on average, FEMA rendered a decision after about 7 months for first appeals, and after about 10 additional months for second appeals. In some cases, the appeal process spanned several years. For example, a subgrantee submitted a first appeal on February 27, 2005, and received an unfavorable response from FEMA on October 20, 2006, an elapsed time of about 20 months. On March 9, 2007, the subgrantee submitted a second appeal and received a response from FEMA 17 months later, on August 7, 2008. In this example, the total elapsed time for the appeal process was about 3 years.[90]

In light of these concerns, some have suggested that arbitration, or other forms of alternative dispute resolution (ADR), may be a more efficient alternative to the traditional appeals process.

---

[84] P.L. 106-390, §204.

[85] The criteria do not appear in regulation or in policy guidance.

[86] 44 C.F.R. §206.437.

[87] 42 U.S.C. §5189a.

[88] For several years the applicant had three appeals. This was reduced, administratively, to two appeals in 1997 to speed up the overall PA process.

[89] Under FEMA regulations, those requesting an appeal have 60 days after they have received notice of the action. Within 90 days after receiving the appeal the regional director (for the first appeal) or the Associate Director (for the second appeal) will notify the appellant of the decision. FEMA may request additional information regarding the appeal in which the appellant has 90 days to provide such information. 44 C.F.R. §206.206(c).

[90] U.S. Department of Homeland Security, Office of Inspector General, *Assessment of FEMA's Public Assistance Program Policies and Procedures,* OIG-10-26. December, 2009, at 5, at http://www.dhs.gov/xoig/assets/mgmtrprts/ OIG_10-26_Dec09.pdf.

In 2009, the American Recovery and Reinvestment Act (ARRA) directed FEMA to establish arbitration panels as an alternative to the traditional administrative appeals process to facilitate resolution of claims arising from Hurricanes Katrina and Rita.[91] On August 31, 2009, FEMA promulgated regulations implementing these arbitration panels.[92]

More generally, Section 1105 of the Sandy Recovery Improvement Act of 2013 directs the Administrator of FEMA to establish a pilot program containing procedures under which an applicant may request the use of alternative dispute resolution. FEMA also has a pre-existing ADR program, under which ADR specialists or mediators use a variety of methods to facilitate an agreement between the parties.[93] Section 1105 specifies that the ADR procedures shall include arbitration by an independent review panel (IRP), but does not appear to preclude other modes of ADR.[94] Nevertheless, the majority of the provision deals specifically with the IRP, suggesting a particular focus on arbitration.

Eligibility for ADR

Under the provision, not every dispute will be eligible for resolution using the ADR procedures to be established under the pilot program. Eligible disputes must involve assistance provided under sections 403,[95] 406,[96] and 407[97] of the Stafford Act. Notably, the new Stafford Act Section 428 (discussed previously) is not part of the list of covered sections. However, because Section 428 of the Stafford Act does not itself authorize any assistance, it is likely that projects approved under Section 428 would still be viewed as providing assistance under the authority of Section 403, 406, or 407 and therefore would not be categorically ineligible for the new ADR procedures.

Disputes must also involve a large enough amount of money to qualify for the pilot program. Specifically, the "legitimate amount in dispute" must be at least $1,000,000, adjusted annually to account for inflation.[98] The phrase "legitimate amount in dispute" is not defined, but suggests that an applicant may not simply allege a disputed amount above $1,000,000 in order to be eligible for ADR. It also suggests that the threshold is measured not by the aggregate size of a particular

---

[91] American Recovery and Reinvestment Act of 2009, P.L. 111-5, §601, providing:

> Notwithstanding any other provision of law, the President shall establish an arbitration panel under the Federal Emergency Management Agency public assistance program to expedite the recovery efforts from Hurricanes Katrina and Rita within the Gulf Coast Region. The arbitration panel shall have sufficient authority regarding the award or denial of disputed public assistance applications for covered hurricane damage under section 403, 406, or 407 of the Robert T. Stafford Disaster Relief and Emergency Assistance Act (42 U.S.C. 5170b, 5172, or 5173) for a project the total amount of which is more than $500,000.

[92] 44 C.F.R. §206.209.

[93] The agency's ADR website notes that ADR can be effective in preventing and resolving disputes involving external parties in many contexts, including disaster projects, hazard mitigation projects, insurance claims and flood mapping, personal injury and property damage claims, rulemaking, contracting, policy development, negotiations, and litigation. FEMA, *ADR Frequently Asked Questions*, Aug. 11, 2010, at http://www2.fema.gov/help/adr/faq.shtm.

[94] For a list of other types of alternative dispute resolution, see Office of Personnel Management, *Alternative Dispute Resolution: A Resource Guide*, at http://www.opm.gov/er/adrguide/section1-a.asp.

[95] 42 U.S.C. §5170b (authorizing essential assistance to meet immediate threats to life and property).

[96] 42 U.S.C. §5172 (authorizing assistance to repair, restore, or relocate damaged public or private non-profit facilities).

[97] 42 U.S.C. §5173 (authorizing assistance for debris clearance).

[98] Inflation would be measured by changes in the Consumer Price Index for all Urban Consumers as published by the Department of Labor.

project, but is limited to the "amount in dispute." In contrast, the arbitration panels for Hurricanes Katrina and Rita PA claims had jurisdiction over disputes involving projects that totaled more than $500,000, even if only a portion of that total was actually disputed.[99]

ADR under the pilot program is also limited to situations where the assistance is provided with a non-federal cost share. Frequently, several types of assistance provided through the Stafford Act are provided under a 100% federal share, especially under section 403 for essential assistance (particularly categories A and B of assistance). Therefore, many claims involving federal assistance may not be eligible for the dispute resolution procedures provided under the pilot program. This provision also restricts eligibility to those projects that have already received a decision on first administrative appeal.[100]

Independent Review Panels

Under the pilot program, several requirements are imposed upon the use of an IRP, presumably in the context of arbitration.[101] The decisions of the IRP will be binding upon both FEMA and the applicant. Additionally, an applicant that has requested an IRP must waive any remaining appeals regarding the dispute. Similar waiver requirements were adopted by regulation when implementing the arbitration panels for Hurricanes Katrina and Rita PA claims established under ARRA.

Section 1105 makes the Administrator responsible for designating a sponsor for the IRPs who must be unaffiliated with the dispute. However, it is explicitly permitted for the sponsor to be another federal agency, an administrative law judge, or a former federal employee. For the arbitration panels for Hurricanes Katrina and Rita PA claims, FEMA had previously used judges that sit on the Civilian Board of Contract Appeals, which oversees disputes between federal agencies and government contractors.[102] The size and composition of the panels is not fixed under Section 1105.

When considering any arbitration scheme, an important question is the appropriate level of review the arbiters would undertake when evaluating disputed determinations made by a federal agency. For example, in one of the first decisions published by the Hurricanes Katrina and Rita PA claims, *Bay St. Louis-Waveland School District*,[103] FEMA argued that the panel's review should be limited to examining whether FEMA's initial determination was either arbitrary or capricious under the APA. Under this standard, the arbiters could not "substitute [their] judgment

---

[99] In the Matter of Forrest County Board of Supervisors, CBCA 1772-FEMA, at 2 (Civilian Bd. Contract App. January 20, 2010) (dispute met cost threshold even though amount in dispute was only $202,443 because total project costs exceeded $500,000).

[100] FEMA regulations provide two levels of administrative appeals regarding assistance determinations. 44 C.F.R. §206.206.

[101] Few requirements beyond the threshold eligibility determination are imposed on ADR methods that do not use an IRP.

[102] Federal Emergency Management Agency, *New Arbitration Panels for FEMA Public Assistance Program Concerning Hurricanes Katrina and Rita*, Aug. 9, 2009, at http://www.fema.gov/news/newsrelease.fema?id=49243.

[103] In the Matter of Bay St. Louis-Waveland School District, CBCA 1739-FEMA (Civilian Bd. Contract App. Dec. 8, 2009).

---

for that of the agency"[104] and would be required to uphold the agency's determination so long as there was no "clear error of judgment."[105]

However, the arbitration panel rejected FEMA's argument and held that its review would be *de novo* and its determination did not need to defer to FEMA's initial findings. In support of this assertion, the panel in *Bay St. Louis-Waveland School District* noted that:

> FEMA's own implementing regulations contemplate that a record *be created specifically for the arbitration panel* which will enable the panel to resolve disputes related to a public assistance grant. The record consists of materials submitted by all parties to the arbitration as well as any independent material from technical and scientific experts that the panel considers necessary to resolve the dispute.[106]

The panel reasoned that its authority to create an independent record would be superfluous if it were to defer to FEMA's initial findings. Therefore, *de novo* review was warranted. Subsequent opinions from arbitration panels have affirmed this conclusion and panels have undertaken *de novo* evaluations of the credibility of witnesses and determinations of feasibility that had previously been made by FEMA officials.

However, such *de novo* review does not appear to be permissible for IRPs established under the new pilot program. Instead, Section 1105 specifically provides that the IRP is limited to consideration of the record at the time of FEMA's decision. Furthermore, a decision of FEMA's may only be set aside if it is found to be arbitrary, capricious, an abuse of discretion, or otherwise not in accordance with law. If FEMA has decided a question of material fact against the claimant during the first appeal, the IRP cannot reverse this finding unless the decision is "clearly erroneous" based on the record available at the time.

Section 1105 also gives IRPs the authority to order a claimant to pay FEMA the costs of arbitration if the request for ADR is found to be frivolous. Amounts received by FEMA under this authority are to be used to credit any appropriations available for eligible assistance, namely the Disaster Relief Fund.

Sunset and Congressional Oversight

Requests for review by an IRP under Section 1105 must be made before the pilot program expires on December 31, 2015. The Comptroller General is also directed to submit a report to the Senate Committee on Homeland Security and Governmental Affairs and the House Committee on Transportation and Infrastructure analyzing the effectiveness of the program. Among other things, the report is specifically directed to discuss:

1. A determination of the available data to complete the report;
2. An assessment of whether the program expedited or delayed the recovery process;

---

[104] Citizens to Preserve Overton Park, Inc. v. Volpe, 401 U.S. 402, 416 (1971).

[105] Ibid.

[106] In the Matter of Bay St. Louis-Waveland School District, CBCA 1739-FEMA, at 7 (Civilian Bd. Contract App. Dec. 8, 2009) (emphasis added).

3. An assessment of whether the program increased or decreased costs;

4. An assessment of the procedures and safeguards established by the IRP and the extent to which such procedures and safeguards were followed;

5. A recommendation on whether any part of the program should be made permanent; and

6. Any other recommendations for modifications to the authority under this subsection.

Strategy for Reducing Costs of Future Disasters

Section 1111 of the Sandy Recovery Improvement Act of 2013 requires the Administrator of FEMA to develop a national strategy "for reducing future costs, loss of life, and injuries associated with extreme disaster events in vulnerable areas of the United States." This strategy will include analysis and recommendations on how the resiliency of the nation can be improved to lessen future disaster loss. This strategy is due to Congress 180 days after enactment (July 28, 2013).

In many regards, this required strategy is very similar to the National Mitigation Framework currently in development, but overdue for release, under Presidential Policy Directive 8: National Preparedness (PPD-8).[107] This Framework will address the capabilities necessary to reduce loss of life and property by lessening the impact of disasters, as well as identifying the roles and responsibilities of for federal, state, and local governments and the private sector in achieving set goals for mitigation.[108] If the final version of the National Mitigation Framework is released, FEMA may consider this reporting requirement fulfilled and would not release an ancillary national strategy.[109]

Applicability to Prior Declared Disasters

The Sandy Recovery Improvement Act of 2013 contains no generally applicable effective date. In the absence of explicit language stating otherwise, the effective date of an enacted provision is presumed to be the day on which it was enacted, January 29, 2013, in this case. It is in keeping with existing practice that the changes in law effectuated by the Act will apply to disasters declared on or after this date. However, it is less clear whether, and to what extent, these provisions will apply to disasters declared before January 29, 2013, although support can be found in the text and legislative history for applying at least some of these amendments to the declarations arising out of Hurricane Sandy.

---

[107] The National Mitigation Framework is one of five National Planning Frameworks called for by PPD-8, the others being for prevention, protection, response, and recovery. The National Disaster Recovery Framework has already been finalized under PPD-8, but the remaining Frameworks are overdue for release/update per the deadline of June 30, 2012, put forth in PPD-8. For more on PPD-8 and its history, see CRS Report R42073, *Presidential Policy Directive 8 and the National Preparedness System: Background and Issues for Congress*, by Jared T. Brown.

[108] For more on the anticipated contents of the National Mitigation Framework, see the working draft Department of Homeland Security, *National Mitigation Framework*, Working Draft, Pre-decisional, May 1, 2012.

[109] Precedent for such is found in the National Disaster Recovery Framework, which the Administration considers fulfilling the requirement for a "National Disaster Recovery Strategy" found in Section 682 of PKEMRA (6 U.S.C. §771).

Provisions That Explicitly Address Prior Declared Disasters

Two of the Act's provisions, sections 1102 and 1104, contain specific language relating to the applicability of those provisions to prior disasters. Section 1102, providing alternative procedures for public assistance projects, explicitly provides that the alternative procedures for public assistance projects will apply to public assistance projects "for which construction ha[d] not yet begun on the date of enactment." It is not specified how the determination of when construction began would be made, potentially leaving FEMA with some interpretive flexibility.

Section 1104, providing streamlined procedures for hazard mitigation assistance, states that its procedures apply to previously declared disasters for which the period for processing requests for assistance has not ended as of January 29, 2013. FEMA regulations require requests for hazard mitigation assistance to be sent within 12 months of the date of a disaster declaration.[110] Extensions can be granted, in 30 to 90 day increments, up to an additional 180 days.[111] The Act does not specify if both of these time frames are to be included in the "period for processing requests for assistance." At a minimum, it likely encompasses the initial 12-month period, placing Hurricane Sandy well within the scope of this provision. It could also be argued that any granted extensions would also be included when determining how far back to apply these new procedures.

Provisions That Do Not Explicitly Address Prior Declared Disasters

While interpreting a statute to have retroactive application in the absence of clear legislative intent is disfavored by the courts, this does not necessarily mean that the provisions of the Act which do not explicitly address applicability will have no effect with respect to disasters that have been declared prior to enactment. The presumption against retroactivity is strongest where application of the new law "would impair rights a party possessed when he acted, increase a party's liability for past conduct, or impose new duties with respect to transactions already completed."[112] However, where these considerations are not present, the Court has upheld retroactive application of laws and regulations to pre-enactment conduct.[113]

It is not clear that the provisions of the Sandy Recovery Improvement Act create the type of retroactive concerns that give rise to the presumption against retroactivity. For example, Section 1103, which authorizes the Administrator to enter into lease arrangements for the purpose of providing temporary housing, would not appear to impair the rights possessed by any party prior to the date of enactment, nor would it increase a party's liability for past conduct or impose new

---

[110] 44 C.F.R. §206.436(d).

[111] 44 C.F.R. §206.436(e).

[112] Landgraf v. USI Film Products, 511 U.S. 244, 280, 114 S. Ct. 1483, 1505, 128 L. Ed. 2d 229 (1994) ("the court's first task is to determine whether Congress has expressly prescribed the statute's proper reach.... When, however, the statute contains no such express command, the court must determine whether the new statute would have retroactive effect, i.e., whether it would impair rights a party possessed when he acted, increase a party's liability for past conduct, or impose new duties with respect to transactions already completed. If the statute would operate retroactively, our traditional presumption teaches that it does not govern absent clear congressional intent favoring such a result.").

[113] For example, Bradley v. School Bd. of Richmond, 416 U.S. 696 (1974) (upholding application of statute authorizing award of attorneys' fees in civil rights litigation to attorneys' services that were rendered prior to the enactment of the statute) and Thorpe v. Housing Authority of Durham, 393 U.S. 268 (1969) (applying eviction procedures promulgated by Department of Housing and Urban Development to pending eviction that had begun before procedures were promulgated).

duties with respect to past transactions. Therefore, it is possible that such leases could be obtained with respect to disasters that had been declared prior to the date of enactment. Additionally, floor statements made by sponsors of the legislation,[114] along with the fact that the relevant division of the Act was entitled the Sandy Recovery Improvement Act, suggest that the enactments made in that division are intended to apply at least to claims arising out of Hurricane Sandy, if not earlier disasters. The same could be said of Section 1105 (directing the Administrator to create an alternative dispute resolution program that includes arbitration before an independent review panel), Section 1106 (directing the establishment of a unified federal review for environmental and historic requirements), Section 1107 (directing the Administrator to review and modify, as necessary, the dollar thresholds for projects to qualify for simplified procedures), Section 1108 (authorizing the President to offer additional forms of assistance), and Section 1109 (directing the Administrator to review and revise individual assistance factors).

Section 1110 (giving tribes the ability to request a major disaster or emergency declaration) also does not explicitly address its applicability to prior declared disasters. Nevertheless, it is unlikely to have any such effect as the tribal request provision will only operate when there has not already been a declaration of an emergency or major disaster in the relevant jurisdiction.

Concluding Observation

The Sandy Recovery Improvement Act of 2013 revised numerous disaster assistance programs authorized by the Stafford Act. Many of these changes will require FEMA to develop policies and regulations to implement the law. For example, as discussed above, FEMA will determine key features of the new alternative procedures for the Public Assistance Program mandated by Section 1102 of the law (within certain statutory guidelines). As of March 7, 2013, FEMA has not released any proposed or final rulemakings to implement these changes, though future rulemakings are anticipated (in addition to those mandated by the law). Therefore, Congress may wish to oversee the implementation of these reforms through hearings or other inquiries to ensure that the changes to the disaster assistance programs align with the future interests of Congress.

---

[114] Rep. Denham, "Sandy Recovery Improvement Act of 2013," House debate, *Congressional Record*, daily edition, vol. 159 (January 14, 2013), p. H68 ("in order to help those communities impacted by Sandy, the FEMA Administrator has made it very clear that these reforms must be signed into law by March 1.").

Appendix. Comparison of the Sandy Recovery Improvement Act of 2013 to the Disaster Recovery Act of 2012

The Sandy Recovery Improvement Act of 2013, as passed by the 113th Congress (P.L. 113-2), included many similar provisions to the Disaster Recovery Act of 2012, as passed by the Senate in the 112th Congress (H.R. 1). The Disaster Recovery Act of 2012 was part of the Senate-passed Disaster Relief Appropriations Act, 2013 that was not taken up for a vote in the 112th House. However, as evidenced by their legislative similarities, it influenced the eventual passage in the 113th Congress.

Table A-1 provides a comparison of how the legislation can be matched, starting from the Sandy Recovery Improvement Act of 2013. Because of the differing structures in the legislation, many of the similarities are not immediately obvious. There were two policy provisions unique to each bill (one each). These provisions are listed at the end of the table. The unique provision of the Sandy Recovery Improvement Act of 2013 is discussed previously in the full report. An explanation of the unique provision of the Disaster Recovery Act of 2012, which did not become law, Section 609(1), is included after the table in this Appendix.

Table A-1. Similar Provisions of the Disaster Recovery Acts

Comparison of Sandy Recovery Improvement Act of 2013 to the Disaster Recovery Act of 2012

Sandy Recovery Improvement Act of 2013	Similar Provision in the Disaster Recovery Act of 2012
Section 1102, Public Assistance Alternative Procedures	Section 609(c)
Section 1103, Federal Assistance to Individuals and Households	Section 609(j)
Section 1104, Hazard Mitigation	Section 609(b)
Section 1105, Dispute Resolution Pilot Program	Section 609(g)
Section 1106, Unified Federal Review	Section 609(f)
Section 1107, Simplified Procedures	Section 609(d)
Section 1108(a), Essential Assistance	Section 609(i)
Section 1108(b), Essential Assistance	Section 609(e)
Section 1109, Individual Assistance Factors	Section 609(h)
Section 1110, Tribal Requests for a Major Disaster or Emergency Declaration under the Stafford Act	Section 609(k)
Section 1111, Recommendations for Reducing Costs of Future Disasters	N/A
N/A	Section 609(1), Report on Impacts to Government Budgets and the Community Disaster Loan Program

Source: CRS analysis of Division B of P.L. 113-2 (113th Cong.), the Sandy Recovery Improvement Act of 2013, and Section 609 of Senate-passed H.R. 1 (112th Cong.), the Disaster Recovery Act of 2012.

Section 609(l) — Report on Impacts to Government Budgets and the Community Disaster Loan Program

Section 609(l) of Senate-passed H.R. 1 (112th Congress) would have required the recently established Hurricane Sandy Rebuilding Task Force[115] to submit a report to various committees of the House and Senate.[116] This provision was not included in the Sandy Recovery Improvement Act of 2013. Among other issues, this report would have evaluated the impact of Hurricane Sandy on local and state budgets, especially the impact on the revenue streams of these governments. The shortage of local revenues, and the resulting limitation on the financial capacity and budget of the local government, has been cited as one of the most significant and consistent hurdles to long-term disaster recovery.[117] The Task Force's report would also have evaluated whether loan assistance is available from private sources to compensate this loss in revenue and impact to their budgets, and whether federal resources and assistance is available to address these budget impacts.

More specifically, the Task Force would have been required to evaluate the ability of FEMA's Community Disaster Loan (CDL) program to "effectively and expeditiously" address these budgetary impacts. The core purpose of the CDL program, currently codified in Section 417 of the Stafford Act (42 U.S.C. §5184, as amended) and administered by FEMA, is to provide financial assistance to local governments that are having difficulty providing government services because of a loss in tax or other revenue following a disaster. The program assists local governments by offering federal loans to compensate for this temporary or permanent loss in local revenue. The program is funded through the Disaster Assistance Direct Loan Program account, rather than the Disaster Relief Fund that funds the majority of other Stafford Act programs. The Task Force was instructed to provide a thorough assessment of the CDL program, to include an analysis of the loan size limitation and FEMA's regulations and procedures governing most aspects of the program.[118] They were also instructed to provide recommendations on how the program could be legislatively amended. If the provision had become law, the report was required within 90 days of enactment.[119]

---

[115] Executive Order 13632, "Establishing the Hurricane Sandy Rebuilding Task Force," 77 *Federal Register* 74341, December 14, 2012, at https://www.federalregister.gov/articles/2012/12/14/2012-30310/establishing-the-hurricane-sandy-rebuilding-task-force.

[116] These committees are the Committee on Appropriations and the Committee on Homeland Security and Governmental Affairs of the Senate, and the Committee on Appropriations and the Committee of Transportation and Infrastructure of the House of Representatives.

[117] U.S. Government Accountability Office, *Disaster Recovery: Past Experiences Offer Insights for Recovering from Hurricanes Ike and Gustav and Other Recent Natural Disasters*, GA0-08-1120, September 2008, p. 17, at http://www.gao.gov/products/GAO-08-1120.

[118] The regulations for the CDL program are found in 44 C.F.R. §206.360-367.

[119] In addition to the provision discussed above, Section 607 of Senate-passed H.R. 1 (112th Cong.) would have changed the cancellation procedures for CDLs issued after Hurricane Katrina. For more on both provisions and the CDL program, see CRS Report R42527, *FEMA's Community Disaster Loan Program: History, Analysis, and Issues for Congress*, by Jared T. Brown.

Author Contact Information

Jared T. Brown
Analyst in Emergency Management and Homeland
Security Policy
jbrown@crs.loc.gov, 7-4918

Francis X. McCarthy
Analyst in Emergency Management Policy
fmccarthy@crs.loc.gov, 7-9533

Edward C. Liu
Legislative Attorney
eliu@crs.loc.gov, 7-9166